Face the Facts
Euthanasia
Linda Jackson

For information, address the publisher:
Raintree, 100 N. LaSalle, Suite 1200, Chicago, IL 60602

Produced for Raintree by Monkey Puzzle Media Ltd.
Printed and bound in China by South China Printing Company.

09 08 07 06 05
10 9 8 7 6 5 4 3 2 1

Library of Congress Cataloging-in-Publication Data
Jackson, Linda, 1964-
    Euthanasia / by Linda Jackson.
        p. cm. -- (Face the facts)
Includes bibliographical references and index.
Contents: Attitudes to death -- A 20th century issue -- Euthanasia today -- Passive euthansia -- Legal euthanasia -- Assisted suicide -- Illegal euthansia -- Case study: Diane Pretty -- Advance directives and living wills -- "Do not resuscitate" orders -- Alternative to euthanasia -- Medical arguments for euthanasia -- Medical arguments against euthanasia -- Ethical arguments for euthanasia -- Slippery slope: ethical arguments against euthanasia -- Cost -- Religion and euthanasia -- Aging and immortality -- Euthanasia campaigners -- How euthanasia affects you.
    ISBN 1-4109-1068-7 (hardcover)
    1. Euthanasia--Juvenile literature. [1. Euthanasia.] I. Title.
    R726.J334 2004
    179.7--dc22
                        2003025693

Acknowledgments
The publisher would like to thank the following for permission to reproduce copyright materials: AKG-Images pp. 30 (Erich Lessing), 40, 41; Alamy p. 4 (The Photolibrary Wales); Associated Press pp. 12 (J R Lavandeira/EFE), 17; Corbis pp. 20 (Amy Powers/The Oakland/Sygma), 21 (Ellis Richard/Sygma), 25 top (William Whitehurst), 31, 44 (Bettmann); Edward Parker Photography p. 8–9; Getty Images pp. 25 bottom (Keith Philpott/Time Life Pictures), 45 (Sandy Huffaker); Kobal Collection p. 43 middle (Highlander Productions); PA Photos pp. 13 (EPA), 16 (EPA), 27 bottom (Chris Ison), 32, 36 (EPA), 49 (Chris Young); Reuters pp. 11 (Aaron Josefczyk), 18 (Will Burgess); Rex Features pp. 22 (Ray Tang), 34–35 (Steve Schneider/SIPA, 38 (Richard Lord); Science Photo Library pp. 42 (James King-Holmes), 46 (Jim Varney); Topham Picturepoint pp. 14–15, 19 (PA), 27 top (PA), 29 (PA); ukActNow p. 6.

Cover photograph reproduced with permission of Science Photo Library (Jesse).

Every effort has been made to contact copyright holders of any material reproduced in this book. Any omissions will be rectified in subsequent printings if notice is given to the publisher.

Some words are shown in bold, **like this**. You can find out what they mean by looking in the glossary.

Contents

Introduction

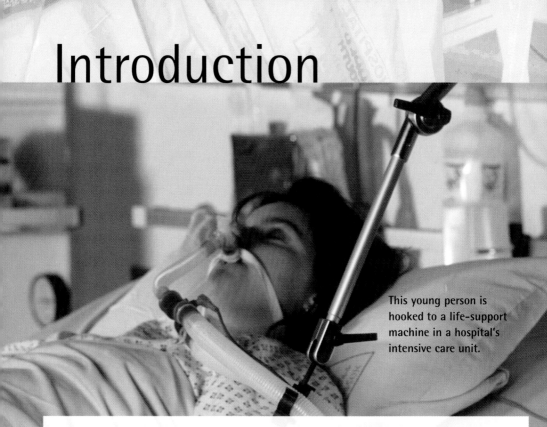

This young person is hooked to a life-support machine in a hospital's intensive care unit.

How would you feel if the person you loved most in the world asked you to help them die?

Euthanasia is the deliberate killing of someone when it is believed that their life is so worthless it should be ended. In most cases it is carried out at the request of the person who wants to die, but sometimes they are unable to make the request and their relatives make it for them. There are several different forms of euthanasia. A brief explanation of these is given in the box on page 7.

Often, euthanasia is referred to as mercy killing—an action that ends unbearable pain, usually being suffered by someone who is **terminally ill** (dying). But many people believe such deliberate killing is murder—they see human life as being **sacred** in all circumstances.

A controversial subject

Euthanasia is a controversial subject that raises fundamental moral questions. For instance, is it ever right to take another individual's life? If it is sometimes right, under what conditions? And, is there any difference between deliberately killing someone (such as by **lethal injection**) and letting them die by withholding treatment (which might mean turning off a life-support machine or not giving artificial nutrition)?

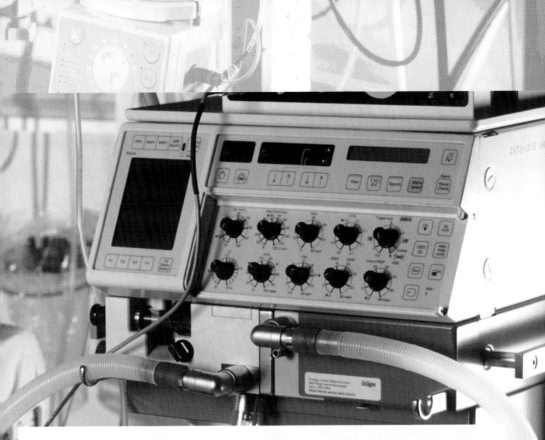

Most of the major religions are opposed to euthanasia, which dates back thousands of years. (The word euthanasia originates from the Greek *eu*, which means "good," and *thanotos*, which means "death.") It is an issue that divides doctors, who swear an oath to do their best for a patient and commit no harm. This may be particularly difficult when they have patients with progressive diseases who are helpless, in constant pain, and want to die.

Euthanasia also arouses powerful emotions among disability groups, who fear that vulnerable people may be regarded by some as a burden on society and be pressured into taking their own lives. It also angers right to life organizations that believe human life must be protected at all costs, even when families want the pain and suffering of their loved ones to end. Some families feel euthanasia is a caring response to a dying person's demands to be put out of their misery.

Suicide tourism

Not all people seeking euthanasia are terminally ill. A new phenomenon—suicide tourists—emerged in 2003. These are people who are in **chronic** pain, but not necessarily dying, who fly to another country where they are helped to die.

❝I want to be able to say goodbye properly to my friends and relatives and have the death of my choice. I do not want to be made to suffer the indignities I have seen my friends endure.**❞**

Steve Barksby, from Manchester, United Kingdom, who has been living with an AIDS diagnosis for the past seven years and has seen many of his friends die from AIDS.

ukActNow.org

At the moment, euthanasia is illegal in every country with the exception of the Netherlands and Belgium. Doctors in the United States (in the state of Oregon) and Switzerland are allowed to help patients commit suicide. During 2003, 42 people died as a result of **physician-assisted suicide** in Oregon. The figure is much higher in Switzerland. Right to die organizations say they helped 300 people take their lives in 2002. But the real number is likely to be far greater. A recent survey suggests up to 31,000 Swiss citizens were helped to die by their doctors.

Legal pressures

Today there are growing pressures around the world both to change the law and to leave it as it is. Due to many scientific breakthroughs, cures are being found for previously incurable diseases. Advanced medical techniques can keep patients alive for much longer than in the past. However, dying is sometimes a long and painful process. As people live longer, world health experts believe the numbers suffering from debilitating conditions such as cancer, heart disease, and other age-related conditions will grow. This is likely to thrust euthanasia into the spotlight, as more people ask for the right to end their own lives as a way to stop their suffering.

Different forms of euthanasia

Active euthanasia—Doctors administer medication knowing that it will shorten a patient's life.

Passive euthanasia—Doctors withhold or withdraw treatment that sustains life. This may mean turning off a machine that is keeping someone alive, or not performing surgery that can extend someone's life for a short time.

Involuntary euthanasia—This occurs without the patient's consent. Another person, such as a close relative, makes the decision on their behalf.

Voluntary euthanasia—This is carried out at the request of the person who dies.

Assisted suicide—When a person provides a patient with the means of killing him or herself. This could mean putting drugs within their reach.

Physician-assisted suicide—When a doctor provides a patient with a prescription of a lethal dose of drugs.

Indirect euthanasia—When a dying patient is given so many painkillers that a side effect is to hasten their death. This can also be referred to as double effect.

Attitudes Toward Death

Dying and attitudes toward suicide have changed dramatically over the last century. In Victorian times, when almost every household had a copy of the Bible, death was regarded as a normal part of daily life. There would be traditional periods of mourning when curtains were drawn and black clothes were worn. Now, as people live longer, healthier lives, dying may occur after a long battle with illness in a nursing home or hospital.

Suicide and euthanasia worldwide

In Japan, the samurai (warriors) considered suicide an honorable method of dying. Elsewhere, there are accounts of tribes and races who abandoned their sick and elderly at the person's wish. Among these are the Inuit (Eskimos). An elder who wished to die would have to ask the community three times before they would assist in his or her suicide.

Early history

The first reference to an act of suicide has been traced back to a stone tablet from ancient Egypt dated around 2000 B.C.E. Later, planned deaths were supported by various Greek philosophers, with both Plato and Aristotle in favor of some form of infanticide (killing of infants) for babies born with deformities.

State-assisted suicide

In ancient Athens, there was a form of state-assisted suicide. People who no longer wished to live stated their reasons

Offerings are made to the dead in this Day of the Dead celebration in Mexico. Special altars, decorated with candles and flowers, are often set up in people's homes. Typical offerings include bone-shaped dough and miniature skulls made of chocolate.

to the Senate, where a magistrate could supply them with hemlock (a plant with deadly poison).

Ancient Rome adopted many Greek ideas, and great compassion was shown to those who were sick or tired of living. Ending one's life to escape unbearable pain was seen as a rational and humane thing to do.

Christian attitudes

Early Christians accepted suicide, which did not become a sin until the 6th century, when laws were passed forbidding Christian burials to anyone who took their own life. This lack of tolerance of suicide continued until the 16th century, when the writings of Roman and Greek philosophers were rediscovered. Sir Thomas More, who in 1516 wrote about an imagined ideal society, believed that euthanasia and suicide were justified for anyone suffering an incurable, painful disease.

Changes to the law

In the 18th century, the traditional belief that suicide was dishonorable continued to be challenged, and laws against attempted suicide were relaxed in France and Prussia. This began a slow process: For example, it took until 1961 before suicide was decriminalized (no longer treated as criminal) in England. Most U.S. states decriminalized suicide after the end of the American Revolutionary War (1783), and all states have decriminalized it since. Suicide is legal in all states in Australia.

A 20th-Century Issue

Although there is evidence that euthanasia was practiced in ancient Greece and Rome, it was only on a small scale. It wasn't until the last part of the 20th century that euthanasia became an issue for society.

In the last 50 years, improvements in medicine have led to large gains in life expectancy. Antibiotics such as penicillin, for example, are products of modern medicine that help prolong life. While people in earlier times died quickly from infectious disease or infections following injuries, antibiotics now often prevent this. Today, most of us can expect to die from **degenerative** (worsening) diseases such as heart disease and cancer.

Figures from the World Health Organization (WHO) show this. In 1900, the average life expectancy for a man in the United States was 47. By the mid-1990s this had risen to 77. This picture is the same throughout the developed world, leading to predictions of an explosion in the number of elderly people. WHO experts believe the impact will be enormous and have warned of a large increase in age-related diseases such as heart disease, cancer, diabetes, and dementia.

Dying itself has changed dramatically. Instead of dying in our own home, surrounded by our family, most of us (80 percent) now die in an institution. This could be in a hospital or nursing home, in a bed next to someone we don't know.

This change from dying quickly at home to dying slowly in a hospital, combined with the medical ability to keep people alive longer, has brought euthanasia to the forefront. More people, faced with a disability and the thought of a prolonged death, now consider euthanasia.

Forecasts

- Some scientists predict that by 2070, female life expectancy in the United States could be as high as 101 years. (The official government forecast for 2070 is only 83.9 years.) Female life expectancy in Japan could reach 100 in 2060, with the United Kingdom reaching the same point in 2085.

- In the United Kingdom, there were more than 300 people aged 100 or more in 1951. By the year 2031, it is estimated this figure will rise to 36,000.

- In 1995, there were less than 9 million people over 65 in the UK. By 2030, there will be 12 million.

- In China, it is estimated that the elderly population could double between 2000 and 2027.

Charlotte Benkner celebrates her 114th birthday in North Lima, Ohio, when she officially became the oldest person in the world in November 2003.

11

Euthanasia Today

Imagine an elderly woman in the advanced stages of cancer who is in so much pain that she cannot even take a sip of water without help. In these circumstances, if she requested it, a **lethal injection** could put an end to her agony. Such an injection would be considered **active euthanasia**.

Active euthanasia

Active euthanasia involves taking action deliberately designed to hasten a person's death. This may involve giving a lethal injection (usually **morphine**), which is viewed by many as a very humane way to die. This action is carried out by someone other than the patient, though nearly always at their request.

Doctors and other health professionals are most likely to take part in active euthanasia, which is illegal in all countries except the Netherlands and Belgium. Medical professionals in other parts of the world who are discovered killing patients in this way face charges of murder or **manslaughter**, even if their patient has requested such a mercy killing.

This form of euthanasia is not the same as **physician-assisted suicide**, in which doctors help a patient to die by putting a lethal dose of drugs within the person's reach. In some instances, doctors may simply provide a prescription for the drugs.

Ramon Sampedro, Spain's leading campaigner for euthanasia, was found dead in a friend's home in Spain. He had been paralyzed from the neck down for 29 years and was the first Spaniard to demand assisted suicide in court. This picture was taken five years before he died.

Cancer sufferer Joy Overell from Queensland, Australia, checks to see if the carbon monoxide level from her car is toxic enough to kill her. She says she will take her own life if the law isn't changed to allow physician-assisted suicide.

Support for active euthanasia is strongest among people who are **terminally ill**, or have incurable conditions. People who seek help to bring about an early death are often people who develop incurable diseases such as AIDS, or sufferers of **ALS** (amyotrophic lateral sclerosis, also known as Lou Gehrig's Disease), a **degenerative** condition that involves the wasting away of the muscles and eventually leads to suffocation from paralysis of the lungs.

Non-requested active euthanasia

Not everyone who experiences active euthanasia is terminally ill. Newborn babies who suffer from potentially fatal complications have been killed through over-sedation. People in the advanced stages of **Alzheimer's disease** or **senile dementia** may also be candidates for active euthanasia if they have previously expressed a wish to die before their disease becomes too extreme.

Passive Euthanasia

Passive euthanasia occurs when a patient dies because medical professionals either don't do something necessary to keep a patient alive, or else stop doing something that is keeping the patient alive. Doctors, for example, might not give life-sustaining drugs or perform a life-saving operation that would extend someone's life. Passive euthanasia may also occur if doctors turn off a life-support machine or disconnect a feeding tube that is the only means of keeping a person alive. These actions may be carried out at the request of a dying person or their legal representative, who is often a family member.

While cases of **active euthanasia** are generally illegal and are relatively rare, acts of passive euthanasia are more widespread. Adult patients have the right to refuse treatment as long as they are seen as competent—in their right mind. For instance, an elderly man dying of lung cancer who catches pneumonia might refuse the antibiotics that could cure his pneumonia.

When treatments can stop

There are occasions in which a person in a deep irreversible **coma** or suffering multiple disabilities is unable to express their will. A patient may have suffered irreversible brain damage, in which he loses his memory, and is unable to think, speak, or to do anything for himself.

In all these circumstances there are strict guidelines regarding the circumstances in which treatments can be discontinued. The guidelines have been created worldwide in the wake of court rulings made over the last fifteen years. Increasingly, doctors consider whether a treatment will provide some benefit to a patient.

Benefits might include the patient's ability to interact with others, to get pleasure from life, or to achieve his or her own goals. If there are no perceived benefits to keeping a patient alive, treatment may be stopped.

Doctors can also withhold resuscitation from seriously ill patients. Bones can be broken during attempts to get the heart beating again. Doctors may feel the lives of patients would be unbearable.

Court rulings

Legal guidance was clarified in the United Kingdom in 1993 when courts ruled that doctors could discontinue artificial feeding by tube. The case involved Tony Bland, who was left in a **persistent vegetative state (PVS)** after the 1989 Hillsborough soccer stadium disaster, in which dozens of soccer fans were killed. Since then, twenty more such patients have been allowed to die in this way.

A soccer fan is carried away after being crushed in the Hillsborough stadium disaster in 1989. Ninety-six Liverpool fans were killed in the incident. Many of the dead were children and teenagers.

Legal Euthanasia

The Netherlands was the first country to pass laws allowing **voluntary euthanasia** (the killing of a person, who is usually **terminally ill**, at their request). For almost 30 years, voluntary euthanasia has been openly practiced by doctors in the Netherlands and carried out thousands of times every year. But it was only in 2002, after a spate of landmark rulings, that mercy killings and **assisted suicides** became legal.

Between 1970 and 1991, numerous court cases involving the deaths of patients at the hands of doctors led to guidelines being published on when euthanasia could be practiced.

Dutch society was generally in favor of euthanasia, and in 2002 the guidelines became enshrined in law. Doctors who are asked to help patients die no longer risk jail if they abide by strict rules. These rules require the patient to make a voluntary and informed request and to be suffering irredeemably (hopelessly). However, it is not a requirement that they are terminally ill. Furthermore, they must have considered all other treatments, sought a second opinion, and be a legal resident of the Netherlands. A similar tolerance to euthanasia is shown in Belgium, where laws permitting euthanasia and assisted suicide were passed just months after the Netherlands made legal history.

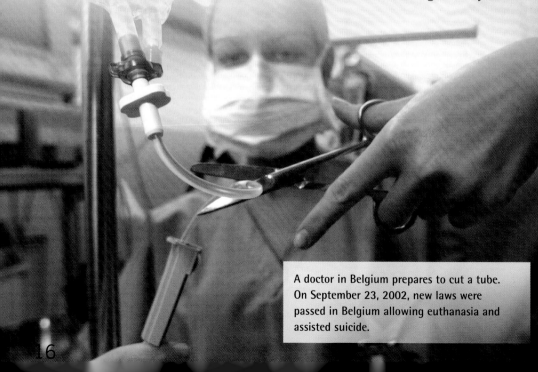

A doctor in Belgium prepares to cut a tube. On September 23, 2002, new laws were passed in Belgium allowing euthanasia and assisted suicide.

Dutch case study

There are an estimated 3,500 euthanasia deaths in the Netherlands every year. For the De Hullu family, death came not once but twice, the second time through euthanasia. In 1961, the De Hullu's six-year-old daughter died of cancer one and a half years after being diagnosed with the disease. In the last few months, her parents and sister watched helplessly as the playful child they knew withered away in bed with not enough strength even to take a sip of water.

Her death was a turning point for the family. After reading about euthanasia in 1977, they all signed a declaration that they would chose euthanasia rather than die such a terrible death. This choice became real in 1991, when Mr. De Hullu was diagnosed with inoperable cancer. He made a decision to have euthanasia when the pain became unbearable. One day, lying on a bed, he told his wife the time had come. She called the doctor, who asked Mr. De Hullu if he was ready to die. He said yes. The doctor prepared a **lethal injection**. Mr. De Hullu said goodbye to his family and then died within minutes of being given the injection.

> **❝I want to be the director of my own life and my own treatment.❞**
>
> Petra Brockmoller, a Dutch woman with cancer who made arrangements for her doctor to kill her. She had undergone 38 treatments for radiation and four of chemotherapy.

Dr. Geertruide Postma is shown at the time of her trial for the killing of her terminally ill mother with a lethal injection. Her mother had asked Dr. Postma to put an end to her life. The Dutch courts gave Dr. Postma a one-week suspended sentence in what became a landmark case.

Assisted Suicide

An **assisted suicide** occurs when a patient is provided with the means to kill themselves. This may involve a doctor prescribing a lethal dose of drugs that are put within the patient's reach. Assisted suicide differs from euthanasia, which involves the deliberate killing of another person.

Australia

Australia was the stage for the first legal act of assisted suicide after the Northern Territory made it legal in 1996. Within months, though, the new laws had been overturned.

Four people were given lethal injections by Dr. Philip Nitschke before the Australian federal government repealed the legislation, which had been widely condemned by church leaders and Aboriginal people (the original inhabitants of Australia). The case put Australia at the center of the euthanasia debate. Nitschke continues to hold workshops to teach people how to kill themselves. Since it is illegal to assist anyone with suicide, he is barely acting within the law.

> ▶Are you aware that if you go ahead to the last screen and press the Yes button you will be given a lethal dose of medications and die?
>
> No   Yes

Dr. Philip Nitschke, a pro-euthanasia campaigner, is pictured with his so-called death machine. Nitschke helped four people die through computer-delivered lethal injections under the short-lived euthanasia laws in Australia's Northern Territory.

Oregon

In the United States, various states tried to pass laws allowing assisted suicide. But only Oregon, where the Death with Dignity Act allows physicians to assist in suicides (**PAS** or **physician-assisted suicide**), made it legal in 1997. Various attempts have been made to overturn the law, but without success. As in the Netherlands, there are strict regulations covering doctors who assist in suicides. Patients requesting help with suicide have to be of sound mind and **terminally ill**. They must also have only six months to live and be a resident of Oregon. Two doctors must agree on the patient's condition before any request is carried out. The three most common reasons patients have given for wanting assisted suicide were the loss of control in their lives, inability to take part in activities they had previously enjoyed, and **incontinence**. One in three felt like a burden on their family and one in four complained of too much pain. Nine in ten had spent time in a nursing home or received **hospice** care.

Switzerland

Assisted suicide is legal in Switzerland as long as nobody profits from a death. The patient does not have to be terminally ill. However, serious ethical questions have been raised about the operations of **Dignitas**, a Swiss assisted suicide group. The group is attracting an increasing number of foreigners who want to take their own lives. More than 100 so-called suicide tourists have flown into the country, where they have been offered lethal drugs by Dignitas volunteers.

Suicide tourist Reginald Crew, 74, flew to Switzerland where he killed himself with the help of volunteers working for Dignitas. Before his death he said he was tired of the constant agony caused by the disease ALS.

Illegal Euthanasia

The so-called Dr. Death, Jack Kevorkian, and his lawyer watch Thomas Youk die. Kevorkian filmed himself giving Youk a lethal injection.

Euthanasia may only be legal in the Netherlands and Belgium, but acts of illegal euthanasia go on around the world. Sometimes these involve doctors and sometimes the patient's family. Anyone caught faces murder or **manslaughter** charges. In some instances, family members have been unable to bear any more suffering and have smothered (suffocated) their loved ones to death. In the majority of cases, it is doctors who are involved in this illegal form of euthanasia. Those that have been caught have ended up in court, and some have been sent to jail.

Dr. Death

In 1999, Dr. Jack Kevorkian was sent to jail in the United States for a minimum of ten years after he videotaped himself giving a **lethal injection** to a patient. The patient was 52-year-old Thomas Youk, a man with **ALS**. Kevorkian, a retired pathologist, sent the videotape to an American prime-time television show. During his trial in Michigan he claimed he had helped up to 130 people die. His imprisonment marked the end of a long battle with the authorities, who had tried to stop him from practicing his own brand of euthanasia. Known popularly as Dr. Death, Kevorkian had practiced his own brand of **physician-assisted suicide** in the state of Michigan for several years. He sought people who wanted to die by advertising himself as a death counselor.

Not Dead Yet

The killings carried out by Kevorkian prompted the founding of Not Dead Yet, a U.S. disability group opposed to **assisted suicide** and euthanasia. The group, which has eleven sister organizations around the world, believes disabled people are being singled out for euthanasia killing because they cost more to treat and care for. Not Dead Yet says some people believe a disabled person's life is worth less than others because they contribute to society in a different way than able-bodied people.

Anti-euthanasia campaigners from Not Dead Yet, a disability rights group, stage a protest.

A fine line

In a 1985 trial in the United Kingdom, a baby with Down Syndrome was rejected by his mother soon after birth. The baby, John Pearson, had a deformed intestine and was severely ill. Dr. Arthur, a highly respected pediatrician (children's doctor), prescribed a **sedative** to stop the child from eating. The child was given water, but no food, and died two days after birth. Dr. Arthur was charged with murder—a charge later reduced to attempted murder. But he was acquitted by a jury, which decided he had not committed an act of **active euthanasia** (deliberate killing)—but had merely prescribed a drug that had resulted in the peaceful death of a child.

Case Study:
Diane Pretty

"The law has taken all my rights away."

Diane Pretty, after failing in her application to the European Court of Human Rights.

ALS sufferer Diane Pretty is pushed by her husband Brian during her legal battle for the right to die. Pretty wanted a guarantee that her husband would not face criminal action if he helped her commit suicide. But the courts ruled against her.

Diane Pretty died two weeks after losing a long battle to allow her husband to help end her life. The 43-year-old British woman was in the advanced stages of **ALS**—a rare condition caused by the breakdown of nerve cells in the brain that control the muscles. She died after suffering breathing difficulties—the very condition she had feared from the start.

The battle for the right to die

Pretty's story made international headlines. She was the first person to go to the European Court of Human Rights and fight for the right to die. She had always said that she wanted her husband to help her die because she feared the choking and asphyxia (suffocation) caused by the disease.

The mother of two took the case to court after the Director of Public Prosecution refused to guarantee that her husband would not be prosecuted if he helped her commit suicide.

Free at last

Pretty died in a nursing home that had cared for her throughout her illness. She was paralyzed from the neck down, **incontinent**, and unable to speak. Her husband Brian had supported her throughout her fight for the right to die. He described her breathing difficulties and how she slipped into unconsciousness:

"The doctors and nurses managed to get her stable for a few days but she was still in pain… They had trouble getting her comfortable and pain-free until Thursday evening after which she slipped into a coma-like state and eventually died.

"Out of all this Diane had to go through the one thing she had foreseen and was afraid of going through and there was nothing I could do to help.

"I was with Diane most of the day and told it was 'time' and then for Diane it was over, free at last."

The case had many implications for relatives of people who are **terminally ill**, since many of these relatives are forced to stand by and watch their loved ones suffer. Like many other countries, suicide is not a crime in the United Kingdom. However, helping someone commit suicide (aiding and abetting) carries a possible jail sentence of up to fourteen years.

Advance Directives and Living Wills

An **advance directive** or **living will** is a legal document that tells a person's doctor what kind of care they would like if they are unable to make decisions or communicate their choices in the future. Without advance directives, some of the most important decisions of a person's life would be left to medical professionals and their family. This could mean patients might be kept alive by artificial means when they might prefer death to treatment, but are unable to speak for themselves.

What advance directives say

Advance directives can take many forms. Most are written by older or seriously ill people. They describe the type of treatment patients want for different levels of illness, including **senile dementia** (which includes Alzheimer's Disease). They usually advise the doctor that a person doesn't want certain types of treatment if they are ill (such as to be put on a **ventilator** if they are in a **coma**). They might also describe their wishes for resuscitation. For example, an elderly patient with heart problems might not want to be resuscitated after a heart attack.

Advance directives can also state that a patient would like a certain treatment no matter how ill they are—although doctors are not obliged to give every possible treatment. They cannot authorize a doctor to do anything unlawful, such as practice euthanasia.

Living will

A living will is one form of advance directive. It only comes into effect when you are **terminally ill**. The document spells out a number of medical scenarios. These range from vegetative state, coma, terminal brain damage, non-terminal brain damage, **chronic** incurable illness, and treatable serious illness. Patients could choose to ask doctors to treat everything in order to prolong life, to try and cure but to regularly review the situation, or provide comfort care such as painkillers only.

> **"Looking back on it, I would like to have let her go that night because ... our Nancy died that night. We've got her body left, but she has no dignity whatsoever."**
>
> Mr. Cruzan, who gave permission for his daughter Nancy to be artificially fed after a car accident in 1983. When he realized her injuries were untreatable, it took a seven-year court battle for her to be allowed to die.

Nancy Cruzan, 25, is pictured in 1983 just months before she was left in a persistent vegetative state (PVS) after a car crash. Her parents fought for artificial feeding to be stopped. But it wasn't until 1990 that the Supreme Court ruled in their favor, outlining the rights of patients or their legal representatives to determine their care. The machines were turned off and Nancy died ten days later.

Do Not Resuscitate Orders

An elderly man lies unconscious on a hospital bed. He is severely ill and has only months to live. Around him is a group of family and medical staff. One question remains: If his breathing or heart stops, should he be resuscitated? It is likely doctors will not resuscitate since the man is already dying. Keeping him alive would only risk causing him greater suffering.

When are DNR orders used?

Such a decision is known in the United States, United Kingdom, and Australia as a **Do Not Resuscitate order**, or **DNR**. They are often seen as a passive form of euthanasia. A DNR order in a patient's file means that a doctor will not be required to resuscitate a patient if their heart stops. They can do this if they believe the patient's heart is unlikely to start beating, if they believe successful resuscitation would lead to a poor quality of life, or if a patient has stated in advance he or she does not want to be resuscitated. Doctors also have to keep in mind that resuscitation can sometimes cause broken ribs, other fractures, ruptured spleen, and brain damage.

DNR and the elderly

Over the last few years, controversy has surrounded the use of DNRs in the United States and United Kingdom. Guidelines issued by doctors' organizations state they should only be issued after discussions with patients or their family. However, there have been cases where seemingly healthy patients discovered they had "do not resuscitate" in their files. This was written without consulting either the patient or their relatives. In the United Kingdom, numerous elderly people found that DNR orders had been written in their files—prompting fears that they would not be revived because of their age. Parents and caregivers of disabled children have also found DNR orders on medical records relating to their children. Since then, doctors have tried to issue clearer guidelines on when DNR orders can be used.

In 2003 the mother of a disabled ten-year-old girl won the right to challenge a London hospital's unlawful refusal to resuscitate her daughter when she experienced severe breathing difficulties. The case in the United Kingdom is expected to become a test case for the rights of the disabled to have the same life-preserving treatment as the able-bodied.

School nurse Bernice "Bunny" Pinnington was fired in the United Kingdom after blowing the whistle on a school's alleged do not resuscitate policy. She had alerted the grandparents of a child at Ysgol Crug Glas special needs school in Swansea, South Wales, about an alleged resuscitation delay order concerning their five-year-old granddaughter in 1998.

This is the medical note of Jill Baker, who was treated for septicemia and cancer at St. Mary's Hospital in Portsmouth, England. She later discovered her medical notes stated she should not be resuscitated in an emergency.

B D Wilson
SHO on CALL
BLEEP 282

In view of underlying diagnosis,
metastatic breast carcinoma and
palliative nature of treatment
In the event of a cardiopulmonary
arrest resuscitation would be inappropriate

NOT FOR SSS

B D Wilson.

Alternatives to Euthanasia

Nursing homes and hospices try to ease the dying process and offer an alternative to euthanasia. The word *hospice* originates from the word *hospitium*. This was the name for part of a monastery where help was given to travelers, the sick, and the poor in the Middle Ages.

Modern hospices

The modern hospice movement began in 1967 with the opening of St. Christopher's Hospice in London by Cicely Saunders. She had been inspired by her work as a nurse and then as a **social worker** to meet the needs of the dying. This included caring for patients' emotional and spiritual needs, as well as their physical needs. She was interested in medical treatments for cancer and had trained as a doctor in her thirties. During the 1960s, she lectured in the United States, where she inspired the hospice movement.

Dying in comfort

Hospice care is based on the belief that death and dying are a natural part of life. It tries to help those who are dying make the most of whatever time is left. Hospices believe that the quality of life should be made as positive as possible.

Care can be offered in specialized **in-patient units**, in nursing homes, in hospitals, or at home. This kind of care can also be known as **palliative care**. Staff, backed by volunteers, do not simply care for patients in the last stages of **terminal illness**. They also specialize in helping people live with illness and death.

Services

As well as specializing in pain control, hospices offer a range of other services. These include nursing, counseling, **physiotherapy**, and **alternative treatments**. The movement also has creative workshops, beauty treatments, and **respite care** for parents of children with life-threatening illnesses. Parents, who often provide 24-hour care, are given a break by respite homes offering temporary care.

The future

Nursing homes and hospices are likely to play an increasingly important role for our aging population. As patients live longer, they may need more treatments to relieve their suffering and improve the quality of their lives.

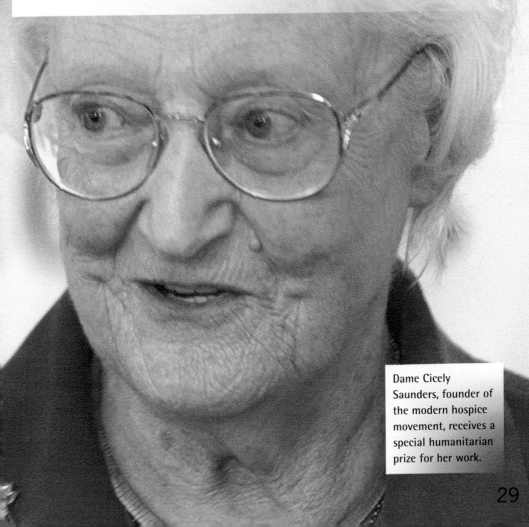

Genetics and euthanasia

In the past, there was little that could be done to manage illness. That is all set to change. Considerable progress in fighting disease has been made in the last 150 years. With new technologies being used to map every human **gene**, scientists hope to better understand the links between genes and disease. Once these have been identified, they plan to develop new precise treatments for diseases that are now incurable. This could make euthanasia unnecessary. However, that time is still many years away. Today, most people can expect to live with at least one **chronic** (long-lasting) disease in their old age, which can be painful and affect their ability to move around.

Dame Cicely Saunders, founder of the modern hospice movement, receives a special humanitarian prize for her work.

29

Medical Arguments for Euthanasia

Some medical professionals who promote **active euthanasia** argue that the right to die is a basic human right. They say patients have told them that they would not want to live in a heavy state of **sedation** to control the pain. And they argue that recent changes in the doctor-patient relationship—from 'doctor knows best' to a more equal relationship—mean that patients should be able to make their own informed decisions.

Support for euthanasia carried out under strict conditions appears to be growing in the United Kingdom. Recently, a survey showed one in seven doctors has secretly killed **terminally ill** patients at their request. Often, this involved an overdose of pain-killing drugs. The doctors who carried out these illegal acts of euthanasia said they were ending the agony endured by some patients (but not all) in their final days. They believe that, for some patients, death is preferable to a life of intolerable suffering. They point to surveys showing that powerful drugs fail to control pain in five percent of cases.

Helping the dying

Another argument for active euthanasia is the risk that terminally ill patients who want to die quickly may feel abandoned by physicians who refuse to help. Polls suggest that almost half of all doctors have been asked by a patient to assist in their suicide or euthanasia.

❝You can find out why it is they feel they need to die and try to make their life more acceptable, but ... you can't provide them with what they really want. You have that sense of failure.❞

Karen Sanders, nurse

This marble bust depicts Hippocrates, the Greek physician, founder of medical science, and father of medicine. He was born in 460 B.C.E. and died in 375 B.C.E.

The Hippocratic Oath, the international code of medical ethics, has become one of the oldest and most binding documents in history. Its principles are held sacred by doctors to this day: Treat the sick to the best of one's ability, preserve patient privacy, and teach the secrets of medicine to the next generation.

Doctors who support active euthanasia have been criticized for breaking their promise not to harm patients. This promise is called the **Hippocratic Oath**. However, doctors who promote assisted suicide say the original Oath, which prohibited killing, also prohibited abortions, surgery, and charging teaching fees. All of these are allowed in certain circumstances. They also say **assisted suicide**, unlike euthanasia, does not involve the ending of life by a physician, as it is the dying person who takes the steps to end their life. Finally, they argue that they swear an oath to relieve all suffering—some interpret this to include

assisted suicide or euthanasia when that is the only way suffering can be relieved.

In the United Kingdom, at least one senior nurse has spoken out in favor of euthanasia. Karen Sanders, who is a senior figure at the Royal College of Nursing (the nurses' professional organization), said she supported euthanasia for incurable and terminally ill patients who consider their lives to be intolerable. Sanders, who specializes in **intensive care** nursing, said she had been asked for help by patients who wanted to end their life—and wasn't able to help them.

31

Medical Arguments Against Euthanasia

The Inquiry is
relatives of s
deceased pati
GP, Harold Fre

In some cases, the
investigate the de
has been written.

NAME   D/
                              DE

Arr   12/

Adk   02/

Harold Shipman (right), the
United Kingdom's worst serial
killer, is shown next to a
newspaper ad (above) that was
published in an attempt to track
down the relatives of more than
80 of Shipman's former patients.

Doctors' professional groups have long
resisted calls for euthanasia and
physician-assisted suicide (PAS) to be
legalized. But they do recognize the
complexities surrounding end-of-life
issues. Strict guidelines have been
drawn up to outline the circumstances
when treatment can be withdrawn
or withheld.

New treatments

Medical arguments against euthanasia
and physician-assisted suicide include
the possibility of misdiagnosis. For
example, there have been cases in which
people have regained consciousness
several years after being misdiagnosed
as being in a **persistent vegetative state**.

Case study Harold Shipman

There is a risk that doctors can abuse their position of power. The potential for this was illustrated when a Public Inquiry examined the crimes of the United Kingdom's worst serial killer, Dr. Harold Shipman (pictured left), who killed himself in prison in 2004. The Inquiry found that Shipman, who was convicted of killing 15 patients, murdered more than 200 others between 1975 and 1998. Many of them were elderly women whom he injected with heroin.

New controls are now in place in the United Kingdom to prevent such crimes. But doctors say controls don't stop abuses. Indeed, there have been a number of cases of **involuntary euthanasia** in the Netherlands, in which doctors have ignored the strict criteria that defines when euthanasia can be performed.

Furthermore, new treatments are being developed all the time. Doctors believe it is wrong to help a patient die if there is a chance he or she could be successfully treated in the future. They argue that some people would not ask for euthanasia if their impending death were painless, and feel money should be spent on better **palliative care** (specialized pain-control for the dying). They fear that if assisted suicide was legalized, some hospitals might not spend money on treatments for the **terminally ill**.

Against a doctor's duty?

Many believe that physician-assisted suicide is fundamentally incompatible with the physician's role as healer. The **Hippocratic Oath** states that doctors should not kill. If exceptions were made, patients could feel abandoned or lose trust in the healthcare system.

Abuse

Major concerns are also raised about how laws allowing euthanasia could be abused. Many health professionals fear that once assisted suicide is accepted for terminally ill adults, it may be permitted for others. This could include people whose lives may be seen as worth less than others, possibly because they have a disability.

Ethical Arguments for Euthanasia

Many people believe that each person has the right to control his or her body and life. Campaigners for **voluntary euthanasia** believe that human beings should have the right to decide when and how to die. A key part of their argument revolves around the fact that suicide is legal almost everywhere. They argue that if it is legal for an able person to kill himself, someone who is disabled through illness should have a similar right to die.

Mercy

Supporters believe it is cruel and inhumane to refuse someone the right to die when they are suffering intolerable pain or distress. It is well known that pain control does not work in all cases. When it doesn't, campaigners say someone should not have to spend their last days suffering.

Regulation

Another argument for legalizing euthanasia is the need to protect vulnerable people. Since euthanasia already occurs, so goes the argument, it is better to make it legal and regulate it properly. Creating a structure to regulate euthanasia would be an improvement on not having any regulations at all. Campaigners want strict safeguards

These volunteers work for Death with Dignity—a group campaigning for the legalization of physician-assisted suicide.

similar to those in Oregon or the Netherlands. They admit the safeguards are not foolproof. However, they argue that some protection against abuse is better than no protection at all.

Moral equivalent

Many people make a moral distinction between **active** and **passive euthanasia**. They believe it is acceptable to withhold treatment and allow a patient to die, but that it is never acceptable to kill a patient by a deliberate act. But supporters of legalizing euthanasia believe there is no real difference. They say the distinction is nonsense, since stopping treatment is a deliberate act, and so is deciding not to carry out a particular treatment. They say the act of removing life support is just as much an act of killing as giving a **lethal injection**. Both acts have the same result—the planned death of a patient on **humanitarian** grounds. Some even go further and say active euthanasia is morally better because it may be quicker and less painful for the patient. It can take days for a patient to die as a result of withholding treatment.

Ethical Arguments Against Euthanasia

If **voluntary euthanasia** became legal, many worry, it would not be long before **involuntary euthanasia** would inevitably occur. Involuntary euthanasia isn't always seen as a bad thing. For example, families may decide an accident victim's life support should be withdrawn. However, there are concerns that involuntary euthanasia would occur in other circumstances. A doctor, for example, might decide not to perform a life-saving operation on a baby born with disabilities.

Opponents to any changes in the laws say they fear that legalized euthanasia could not be kept under control. They believe doctors could start killing patients without asking their permission.

These patients could include the vulnerable or elderly. Indeed, groups representing disabled people believe euthanasia would lead to some lives being worth more than others. It is feared that the lives of disabled people would be seen as less valuable than the lives of the able-bodied. Families or

Case study   Nazi euthanasia

Groups campaigning for the rights of people with disabilities say history shows the extreme consequences of euthanasia. In the 1930s, the Nazis in Germany engaged in massive programs of involuntary euthanasia. This was part of Hitler's attempt to establish a German master race. Children born with physical deformities or mental problems were systematically killed. Adults with disabilities were also killed. Later, the program became part of the Holocaust (mass extermination of Jews).

Annemarie D.

Children walk through an Austrian cemetery showing the pictures of hundreds of children with disabilities killed as part of a Nazi involuntary euthanasia program in the 1930s and 1940s. A special burial service was held for the 772 youngsters who were killed at a clinic in Vienna.

caregivers of vulnerable people might see them as an intolerable burden and place subtle pressure on them to end their lives.

Too much power to doctors

Another argument against euthanasia is that it would give too much power to doctors. It is doctors who give patients the information on which they will base their decisions about euthanasia. Some people say that any legalization of euthanasia, no matter how strictly regulated, would put doctors in an unacceptable position of power. Some doctors have defied guidelines and made these decisions improperly. Evidence shows that some doctors put **Do Not Resuscitate orders** in the files of elderly patients without consulting them or their families. Furthermore, in the United States, DNR orders are more commonly used for African-Americans, alcohol abusers, non-English speakers, and people infected with **HIV (Human Immunodeficiency Virus)**. This suggests that doctors have stereotypes (fixed ideas) of who is not worth saving.

37

Counting the Cost

A nurse cares for a premature baby who is being kept alive in an incubator.

Cost of treating the elderly in the United States:

Large sums of money are spent on treating elderly people in the United States. Almost one in three dollars of government money earmarked for the poorest elderly patients is spent on their last year of life. One in every 10 dollars spent on elderly patients is on the last 40 days of life.

Cost of treating terminally ill in the United Kingdom:

A **terminally ill** person may spend more than ten months in a hospital ward, unfit to return home without support. At $200 per day this costs the National Health Service in the United Kingdom more than $60,000. In addition, the hospital must find sufficient funds to give appropriate medical treatment.

Doctors and hospitals have to make difficult choices concerning healthcare. They have a limited amount of cash to spend and increasing numbers of patients to care for. This means they can't always provide the type of care or treatment patients would like to receive.

This rising pressure on budgets has led to fears that euthanasia or **assisted suicide** could become a cheap solution to healthcare. A **lethal injection** costs approximately $35 to $45, making it far cheaper than providing medical care. In the United States, it is estimated that the annual cost of caring for 25,000 adults in **persistent vegetative state (PVS)** is between one and seven billion dollars every year. The annual cost of looking after a PVS patient in a nursing home is estimated to be as much as $180,000.

The doctors' dilemma

Important questions are raised by the cost of treatments for some conditions. Doctors and healthcare providers also have to consider if it is ethical to engage in extremely expensive treatment of terminally ill people in order to extend their lives by a few weeks, especially if it is against their will. The money used in this way is then not available for pre-natal (before birth) care or infant care, where it would save lives and significantly improve the long-term quality of life for others.

The United States

Studies show that millions of Americans have no medical insurance. As a result, the elderly, the poor, and minorities often have no easy access to treatment or pain control. The insurance-based health system complicates the euthanasia debate, however, because of the central role of the health maintenance organizations (HMOs) to which most people belong. These agencies seek to keep costs down by limiting patients' choice of doctors and treatments and by bargaining down the price of medical supplies. If euthanasia were legalized, there would be suspicion that HMOs—possibly through doctors—were influencing the decisions of seriously ill or disabled people. It would be more cost-efficient to have patients die rather than receive long-term care.

Religion and Euthanasia

Death is a major issue for religions. All faiths try to offer a meaning for dying, which is often seen as a spiritual process. They have strong views on euthanasia because of this. Almost all the major religions are against euthanasia. Human life is seen as a gift and **sacred**. However, some religions accept there are circumstances when **passive euthanasia** may be justified.

The Christian view

Most Christians are against euthanasia, seeing human life as a gift from God. They feel no human being should have the power to take life away from another. There is also a belief that all human beings are equally valuable in the eyes of God. However, some Christians accept that euthanasia is acceptable in some circumstances. Others, including members of the Roman Catholic Church, see euthanasia as morally wrong. The Roman Catholic Church believes life has a value, whatever form that takes. Suffering and pain are not reasons to end life.

The Jewish view

Judaism teaches that all human life is sacred. Furthermore, Jewish laws teach that it is wrong for anyone to shorten human life. However, there are circumstances in which the faith allows doctors to withhold or withdraw treatment, if the treatment is delaying

Moses holds a tablet of stone containing the Ten Commandments, which have been a basis of morality for the last 3,000 years. He is a highly influential prophet in Judaism, Christianity, and Islam. The Bible says Moses spent 40 years in the wilderness before God appeared to him from a burning bush.

the dying process. This might include withholding medication to someone who only has 72 hours to live.

Islam

Muslims are against euthanasia, believing all life is sacred since it is given by Allah, and Allah chooses how long each person should live. Suicide and euthanasia are not listed as acceptable reasons for death in the teachings of the Islamic holy book, the Quran. This says life must not be taken except in the "course of justice." It goes on to explain that lives can be taken during war or as a punishment for a crime.

Hinduism

Hindus believe in the **reincarnation** of the soul through many lives—not necessarily all human. A soul's next life is decided as the consequence of its

own good or bad actions in previous lives. Most Hindus would say that a doctor should not accept a patient's request for euthanasia since this will cause the soul and body to be separated at an unnatural time. Others believe that euthanasia cannot be allowed because it contradicts the teaching of doing no harm.

Buddhism

Most Buddhists believe that **voluntary euthanasia** is wrong. Buddhism places great importance on non-harm and on avoiding the ending of life. As with Hinduism, death is seen as a transition, with the deceased person being born to a new life. The intentional ending of life is against Buddhist teaching.

This statue depicts Buddha. He was born a prince in the 6th century B.C.E., but turned his back on privilege and power in an attempt to discover the fundamental truths of life and to find enlightenment.

Aging and Immortality

Scientific advances, which have led to people living longer, are predicted to continue well into the next century. Population forecasters expect the life expectancy of girls born in 2070 to be over 100. By 2020, the number of people in the world over the age of 65 is expected to almost double—from 380 million now to 690 million. The use of new technologies to identify every human **gene** is already leading to the development of new drugs. These, in turn, may cure diseases associated with aging. Indeed, recent research findings suggest aging is not a random wearing out of the human body. Rather, it appears to be controlled by specific genetic change.

Scientists are now trying to identify genes related to the progression of a disease. These can then be used as a target to develop drugs against the disease. They have already identified rogue genes in cases of breast cancer.

High life expectancy

Experts in medical ethics believe these scientific advances could lead to people living well beyond the age of

This computer screen displays a human DNA (deoxyribonucleic acid) sequence. Genes, which are the basic units of heredity, are made from a segment of DNA. Each person has thousands of genes that make up individual characteristics (genetic traits). Scientists hope that by learning more about human genes they will be able to develop new drugs that will help to cure illnesses caused by genetic change.

120 years—the oldest that people tend to currently live. They predict this technology would be expensive. It would also create the terrifying prospect of so-called immortals, who were wealthy enough to afford life-extending treatment, living side by side with mortals. We have already seen this happening in literature and movies. (The movie *Highlander*, for example, tells the story of Connor MacLeod, an immortal who wanted to grow old with his wife.) Medical ethicists believe immortality (living forever) could become a reality. They say society needs to examine now how we will live with the prospect.

If this theory came true, we may eventually begin to question how long we want to live. Even today, many elderly people say they are tired of life. The prospect of immortality raises questions: What would it be like to live forever? Would it be fun or boring? What would it be like to stay alive once all your friends had died? Faced with the prospect of life going on forever, people might see euthanasia as offering a dignified end.

A scene from the movie Highlander (1986) featuring the actor Christopher Lambert.

Euthanasia Campaigners

In 1935, a group of doctors, lawyers, and clergymen in the United Kingdom set up the Voluntary Euthanasia Society. Three years later, a similar group was set up in the United States, and one followed in Canada in 1980. However, the British and U.S. groups were very small and insignificant for three decades after their formation. But after the highly publicized Karen Ann Quinlan right to die case in New Jersey in 1976, the movements became more vocal. The Quinlan case highlighted how life in a **persistent vegetative state** could be extended indefinitely.

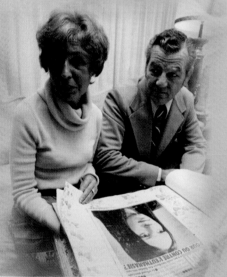

The parents of Karen Ann Quinlan examine the cover of a magazine that makes up part of a scrapbook of their daughter's life. The photograph was taken two years after Karen Ann fell into a coma. She died eight years later after never regaining consciousness.

Case Study
Karen Ann Quinlan

Karen Ann Quinlan was the first person at the center of the right to die debate in the United States. The 21-year-old Quinlan collapsed after using alcohol and drugs at a party in 1975. Doctors saved her life, but she suffered brain damage and lapsed into a persistent vegetative state. Her family waged a legal battle for the right to remove her life-support machine. They succeeded, but in a final twist Quinlan kept breathing after the respirator was unplugged. She remained in a **coma** for almost ten years in a New Jersey nursing home until her death in 1985.

Members of the Californian Right to Life Coalition protest against a meeting of the Hemlock Society, which campaigns for the legalization of voluntary euthanasia.

Pro-euthanasia groups

The campaign for legalizing euthanasia stretches far and wide. Some groups campaign to make it legal for a competent adult (who is suffering unbearably from a **terminal illness**) to be allowed to request medical help to die.

Other groups campaign for changes in the law so that dying patients can choose a peaceful death as part of the care given to them as they reach the end of life.

Anti-euthanasia groups

There are many opponents to the legalization of euthanasia. For example, the International Task Force on Euthanasia and **Assisted Suicide** is an international group opposed to assisted suicide and euthanasia. The goal of the International Task Force is to ensure that a patient's right to receive care and compassion is not replaced by a doctor's duty to prescribe poison or administer a **lethal injection** when asked.

How Euthanasia Affects You

Sooner or later, everyone has firsthand experience of the death of a loved one. It might be a family member or a friend. If this death is long and painful, it is very distressing. Those left behind feel hopeless, helpless, and confused. At times like this people might start considering the arguments for and against euthanasia.

They might go to a public library for further information on the subject. They could have a chance to voice their opinions during school debates, since euthanasia is often discussed in school classes. Those who feel very strongly about the subject may decide to join a group that campaigns for or against legalizing euthanasia.

A boy is counseled by a woman who has been specially trained to give advice and support in times of emotional distress.

Preparing for a death

Any death of a family member or friend leaves people with a sense of **bereavement**. If the death is the result of some form of euthanasia, dealing with the death can be even more difficult. At times like this, people can reach out for support to specially trained counselors or **social workers**. These people are trained to answer all types of questions, and can be helpful during the dying process. For example, they can explain why a dying relative, who loved food, has now lost their appetite. (This is normal in advanced stages of illness.) A person might be left feeling angry, or sad, or even guilty that someone they love is dying, or has chosen to die early through euthanasia. Counselors will reassure people that these are normal feelings that won't last forever.

Supporting the dying

Some people may find it difficult to face their sick loved ones, who need contact more than ever at this time. It is not unusual for a person to deny that someone they love is dying. They can find it particularly difficult and may feel abandoned or hurt if their relative has opted for euthanasia. Others may feel relief that their loved one has chosen to end their suffering through euthanasia rather than let nature take its course. Counselors believe any difficulties can be overcome if a person learns more about the illness and recognizes death is inevitable and is part of the cycle of life. Counselors will stress the importance of staying in touch with a dying relative or friend. It can give the person a chance to discuss anything they are worried about. This could include their reasons for choosing a form of euthanasia.

Support after death

Bereavement counseling can help a person come to terms with their grief after a loved one has died. Family doctors, nurses, and a person's religious community can all offer continued support after the death of a loved one. Help is also available to people who are struggling to cope with the loss of a relative or friend through euthanasia. A number of organizations offer special support to children who have lost a parent.

Conclusion

Today, euthanasia is in the spotlight more than ever. Medical advances and the aging population of many Western countries mean more and more people may be faced with a choice between choosing medical treatment and illness, or death through mercy killing. Over the last 50 years, people have started examining their rights and, as society changes its view of death, a growing number are calling for the right to die.

Legal opinions

In recent years, the push for legalization of **voluntary euthanasia** and **physician-assisted suicide** has strengthened, gaining ground in some cases and losing ground in others. The European Court of Human Rights ruled in April 2002 that there is no right to die. The U.S. Supreme Court has also ruled that Americans have no constitutional right to die. This means that any state considering legalizing euthanasia or **assisted suicide** could only allow it in certain circumstances under strict criteria.

Public opinion

Over the last 40 years, poll after poll shows public opinion has shifted in favor of euthanasia as life expectancies increase. A typical survey question, between 1973 and 1995, is: "Do you think a patient who is **terminally ill**, with no cure in sight, should have the right be put out of his or her misery, or do you think this is wrong?" In 1973, 37 percent of respondents said the patient should have the right to be put out of misery, and 53 percent said this was wrong (10 percent said they didn't know). In 2003, the numbers changed dramatically: 61 percent said that patient should have the right to die, and 36 percent said this was wrong. In a 2001 poll, six in ten Americans said the United States government should not overturn Oregon's Death with Dignity Act. The reason for this remarkable shift in opinion is not known. Medical associations and politicians generally remain opposed to euthanasia, although their opposition has softened.

The future

The battle for the right to die is likely to continue. Scientists predict that by the year 2070 the average life expectancy will rise to 101 in wealthier countries. It is likely to be as early as 2060 in Japan. As we have seen, there are powerful arguments for and against euthanasia. But what happens next will depend on public opinion, and the discovery of treatments for age-related diseases and improvements in **palliative care**.

These protesters are demanding a change in the law to allow euthanasia in certain circumstances. The petition, which was organized by campaign group ukActNow, was signed by 50,000 people with terminal illnesses. They want the law to allow them the right to choose to die with the aid of medical assistance.

Facts and Figures

Care costs

In 2003, a unit of blood cost between $225-$275, and several units may be required per week by a patient suffering from, for example, chronic anemia. This may be caused by internal bleeding from an ulcer, or any prolonged illness and extended treatment. For a person with prostate cancer, typical drugs cost $230 per month.

Hospices

Today, there are more than 2,300 hospice programs in the United States. These programs cared for more than 600,000 people in the United States in 2003. There are more than 250 hospices in the United Kingdom.

Deaths

World Health Organization figures show cancer, heart disease, and other **chronic** conditions kill more than 24 million people a year worldwide. This is 47 percent of the annual global total deaths from all causes.

Circulatory diseases such as heart attacks and strokes kill 15.3 million a year.

Cancer in all forms kills 6.3 million a year.

Lung disease kills 2.9 million a year.

Euthanasia deaths in the Netherlands

The Netherlands has a population of approximately 15 million. In 1990, there were 135,000 deaths. Of these, 11,000 were a result of **active euthanasia**, **physician-assisted suicide**, or overdoses of painkilling drugs. On top of this, there were almost 12,000 deaths due to **passive euthanasia** involving the withdrawal or withholding of treatment.

Suicide

In the United States, an estimated 30,000 people commit suicide every year. Roughly 4,000 young people (between the ages of 15 and 24) and more than 5,000 elderly Americans (age 65 and older) commit suicide every year.

Forecasts

In 2020, at least 15 million people worldwide will develop cancer compared with 10 million now, largely as a result of people living longer.

Between 1995 and 2025, the number of people with diabetes is expected to rise from 135 million to 300 million worldwide.

By 2020, the number of people over the age of 65 is expected to rise from 380 million to 690 million worldwide.

There is likely to be a large increase in cases of **senile dementia** (loss of intellectual functions, such as thinking, memory, and reasoning). It is estimated that 29 million people already suffer from it. By the year 2025, forecasters are predicting that, due to improvements in medicine which will lead to increased life expectancy, Africa, Asia, and Latin America could have more than 80 million sufferers combined.

Further Information

Contacts in the United States

ALS Association
27001 Agoura Road, Suite 150
Calabasas Hills, CA 91301-5104
This association offers a range of resources to sufferers and their families.

Alzheimer's Association
919 N Michigan Avenue, Suite 1000
Chicago, IL
The organization conducts research and offers support to people living with Alzheimer's disease.

Care-Givers USA
c/o The Oakton Press Inc.
11350 Random Hills Road, Suite 650
Fairfax, VA 22030
This organization supports care-givers.

National Hospice of Palliative Care Organization (NHPCO)
1700 Diagonal Road, Suite 625
Alexandria, VA 22314
The foundation offers information in support of hospices.

National Library of Medicine
8600 Rockville Pike
Bethesda, MD 20894
This resource has a great deal of information on AIDS.

Contacts in Australia and New Zealand

Australian Cancer Society
PO Box 84, Jamison Centre,
ACT 2614, Australia
This society gives support and information to cancer sufferers and their families.

Cancer Society of New Zealand
PO Box 10847 Wellington
Cancer Society staff and volunteers provide support and information for people with cancer and for their families. Associated with each regional cancer society are support groups; they also know of other groups to do with breast cancer and provide information and availability about therapies.

Further reading

Dworkin, Gerald, et al, *For & Against: Euthanasia and Physician-Assisted Suicide*. (Cambridge: Cambridge University Press, 1998).

Torr, James D, *Opposing Viewpoints: Euthanasia*. (San Diego: Greenhaven Press, 2000).

The following book is suitable for older readers:

Humphry, Derek, *Final Exit: the Practicalities of Self-Deliverance and Assisted Suicide for the Dying*.(Los Alamitos: Delta, 2002).

Glossary

active euthanasia
when a person directly and deliberately causes a patient's death. The person may be a doctor, a relative, or a friend.

advance directive
legal document that tells doctors what kind of treatment you would like if you were unable to communicate for yourself

ALS (amyotrophic lateral sclerosis)
neurodegenerative disease resulting in progressive weakness of voluntary muscles throughout the body. There is currently no known cure for ALS (also known as Lou Gehrig's Disease).

alternative treatments
medical treatments that are unusual and are only used by a minority of people

Alzheimer's disease
degeneration of the brain, resulting in impaired memory, thinking, and behavior

assisted suicide
when a person who wants to die needs help and is given the means to kill themselves, often by a prescription for a lethal dose of drugs

bereavement
being deprived of someone valued, especially as a result of death

chronic
word describing a recurrent disease that goes on for years

coma
extended period of unconsciousness

degenerative
having a wasting effect

Dignitas
Swiss right to die organization that offers assisted suicide

Do Not Resuscitate orders
instructions telling medical staff not to attempt to resuscitate a patient if the patient has a heart attack or stops breathing

gene
chemical information received by children from their parents. Each gene controls one aspect of development.

Hippocratic Oath
promise made by doctors to do everything they can to preserve life

HIV (Human Immunodeficiency Virus)
virus which causes AIDS

Holocaust
killing of Jews and others by the Nazis before and during World War II

hospice care
specialized care for the terminally ill

humanitarian
concerned with human welfare, and designed to reduce suffering

incontinence
loss of control over bodily functions

indirect euthanasia
providing treatment that has the predicted side effect of shortening a patient's life

in-patient unit
where patients stay overnight

intensive care
continuous treatment provided in a hospital for patients who are seriously ill

involuntary euthanasia
euthanasia without the patient's consent

lethal injection
putting a poisonous substance into the body in order to cause death

living will
type of advance directive that explains what treatment a person wants at the end of his or her life

manslaughter
unintentional unlawful killing

morphine
powerful drug used to relieve severe pain

Nazis
members of the Fascist National Socialist Workers' Party who, led by Adolf Hitler, controlled Germany from 1933 to 1945

palliative care
total care of incurably ill patients

passive euthanasia
withdrawing or withholding treatment that leads to the death of a patient. This might include stopping artificial feeding or turning off a life-support machine.

persistent vegetative state (PVS)
often referred to as brain-death. Involves the loss of higher brain functions. PVS patients have lost their thinking abilities and awareness of their surroundings, but have periods of apparent wakefulness and sleep patterns.

physician-assisted suicide (PAS)
when a doctor prescribes a lethal dose of medication

physiotherapy
treatment of stiffness or muscle weakness by moving the affected parts

reincarnation
belief that, after death, the soul is reborn in another body

respite care
caring for sick people for short periods in order to give their caregivers a break

sacred
safeguarded, protected, regarded as holy

sedative
drug used to calm or sedate

senile dementia
disease of old age that includes loss of memory (also referred to as Alzheimer's Disease)

social worker
person who provides support and help to vulnerable people

terminal illness
illness that leads to a life expectancy of not more than twelve months

ventilator
artificial breathing apparatus

voluntary euthanasia
euthanasia carried out at the request of the patient

Index